How To Raise Your Credit Score

# How To Raise Your Credit Score

## What The Banks Not Telling You

### Alwyn Bishop

# HOW TO RAISE YOUR CREDIT SCORE

**Copyright 2018 by Author - All rights reserved.**

This document is geared towards providing exact and reliable information in regards to the topic and issue covered. The publication is sold with the idea that the publisher is not required to render accounting, officially permitted, or otherwise, qualified services. If advice is necessary, legal or professional, a practiced individual in the profession should be ordered.

- From a Declaration of Principles which was accepted and approved equally by a Committee of the American Bar Association and a Committee of Publishers and Associations.

In no way is it legal to reproduce, duplicate, or transmit any part of this document in either electronic means or in printed format. Recording of this publication is strictly prohibited and any storage of this document is not allowed unless with written permission from the publisher. All rights reserved.

The information provided herein is stated to be truthful and consistent, in that any liability, in terms of inattention or otherwise, by any usage or abuse of any policies, processes, or directions contained within is the solitary and utter responsibility of the recipient reader. Under no circumstances will any legal responsibility or blame be held against the publisher for any reparation, damages, or monetary loss due to the information herein, either directly or indirectly.

Respective authors own all copyrights not held by the publisher.

The information herein is offered for informational purposes solely, and is universal as so. The presentation of the information is without contract or any type of guarantee assurance.

The trademarks that are used are without any consent, and the publication of the trademark is without permission or backing by the trademark owner. All trademarks and brands within this book are for

# How To Raise Your Credit Score

clarifying purposes only and are the owned by the owners themselves, not affiliated with this document.

# How To Raise Your Credit Score

# Table of Contents:

## CHAPTER 1: INTRODUCTION TO CREDIT SCORE

| | |
|---|---|
| **INTRODUCTION:** | **7** |
| **10 SECRETS TO BETTER MORTGAGE RATES BANKS NEVER TELL YOU:** | **8** |
| **CREDIT SCORES CALCULATION FACTORS** | **13** |
| • Punctuality of payments | 13 |
| • Capacity used | 14 |
| • Length of credit history | 14 |
| • Types of credit used | 14 |
| • Recent search for credit or the amount of credit obtained recently | 14 |
| **CRITERIA NOT INCLUDED IN CALCULATION OF CREDIT SCORE** | **17** |
| **5 THINGS TO BOOST YOUR CREDIT SCORE:** | **17** |
| **WHAT IS CREDIT SCORE?** | **18** |
| **HOW IS CREDIT SCORE CALCULATED?** | **19** |
| **INSTALLMENT HISTORY (35%)** | **19** |
| **MAKE INSTALLMENTS ON TIME** | **19** |
| **WHAT DAMAGES CREDIT AND HOW IT CAN PREVENT** | **22** |
| **DAMAGING MYTHS:** | **22** |
| Myth # 1: | 22 |
| Myth # 2: | 22 |
| Myth # 3: | 23 |
| Myth # 4: | 24 |

## CHAPTER 2: WHY YOUR CREDIT SCORE MATTERS

| | |
|---|---|
| **HOW YOUR CREDIT SCORE AFFECTS YOU** | **29** |

## CHAPTER 3: HOW CREDIT SCORING WORKS

## CHAPTER 4: IMPROVING YOUR SCORE–THE RIGHT WAY 5

# How To Raise Your Credit Score

| | |
|---|---|
| **IMPROVE YOUR PAYMENT HISTORY** | **40** |
| **DECREASE OUTSTANDING DEBTS** | **40** |
| **GET A BETTER HISTORY** | **41** |
| **MANAGE CREDIT EFFECTIVELY** | **41** |
| **KEEP A PROPER MIX OF THE RIGHT RESULTS** | **41** |

## CHAPTER 5: COPING WITH A CREDIT CRISIS

## CHAPTER 6: REBUILDING YOUR SCORE AFTER A CREDIT DISASTER

| | |
|---|---|
| **PART 1: CREDIT REPORT REPAIR** | **47** |
| **KNOW YOUR RIGHTS** | **49** |
| **ORGANIZE YOUR ATTACK:** | **49** |
| Unpaid Debts And Collections: | 50 |
| Statutes Of Limitations: | 50 |
| Should You Pay Old Debts? | 51 |
| A Couple More Things To Remember: | 51 |
| **PART 2: ADDING POSITIVE INFORMATION TO YOUR FILE** | **52** |
| BECOME AN AUTHORIZED USER OF A CREDIT CARD : | 52 |
| GET CREDIT OR CHARGE CARDS IF YOU DON'T HAVE ANY: | 52 |
| GET AN INSTALLMENT LOAN: | 53 |
| **PART 3: USE YOUR CREDIT WELL** | **53** |

## CHAPTER 7: IDENTITY THEFT AND YOUR CREDIT

## CHAPTER 8: FIXING YOUR CREDIT SCORE FAST

| | |
|---|---|
| **HOW TO FIX YOUR CREDIT YOURSELF** | **61** |
| **WHAT AM I LOOKING FOR PRECISELY?** | **61** |
| **WHAT STEPS SHOULD I PERFORM TO CORRECT THESE ACCOUNTS?** | **61** |
| **WHAT SHOULD GO ON A CREDIT ARGUMENT CORRESPONDENCE LETTER AND WHY I AM WRITING IT?** | **62** |
| **HOW WILL A CORRESPONDENCE ASSIST ME TO REPAIR MY CREDIT?** | **62** |

# How To Raise Your Credit Score

## CHAPTER 9: INSURANCE AND YOUR CREDIT SCORE

## CHAPTER 10: WHAT WILL BAD CREDIT COST YOU

| | |
|---|---|
| How Much Does Bad Credit Cost? | 71 |
| Some things to ponder on | 72 |
| Difference Between Good Credit And Bad | 73 |
| 5 things to determine what is a bad credit score versus a good score | 77 |

## CHAPTER 11: KEEPING YOUR SCORE HEALTHY

| | | |
|---|---|---|
| 1. | Pay Your Bills On Time | 80 |
| 2. | Don't Apply for Credit Unless You Need | 81 |
| 3. | Keep Your Balances Low | 81 |
| 4. | Don't Apply for a lot of New Credit in a Short Period of Time | 81 |

## CONCLUSION

# Chapter 1: Introduction To Credit Score

## Introduction:

Your credit score (also known as a credit rating) plays a big role in your financial well being. That's why checking your credit score, and understanding the factors that affect it, is a great way to take control of your financial future. Your credit score can have an impact on most of your finances. From being accepted for a credit card, mobile phone contract or mortgage, to even the type of home broadband deal you're offered. One thing is clear: the better your credit score, the healthier your finances and the more likely you are to be accepted for credit

When I first started writing about credit scores more than a decade ago, few people knew what these three-digit numbers were or how they worked. Today most people have at least a vague understanding that credit score is important. But they often don't realize how important—until they get turned down for a loan or an apartment, or wind up paying more interest or higher insurance premiums than they expected.

The credit crunch, financial crisis, and recession just made matters worse. It split the world into two, with one set of rules for the credit "haves" and another for the "have-nots." People with good credit scores have enjoyed some of the cheapest loans in a generation. Lenders still fight for their business and reward them with low rates. It's a very different world for people who don't have good scores.

Lenders who once encouraged their business now slam the doors. Banks and credit card issuers burned by the recession have grown weary of taking any risk at all. Unfortunately, more people every day fall into the group of credit have not as high unemployment and the foreclosure crisis take their tolls. These folks desperately need to know how to rehabilitate their battered scores but are often given bad or misleading advice about how to do so. People's hunger to learn about credit scoring helped make previous editions of this book into national best-sellers. The book you have in your hands now has been completely updated to reflect current laws, trends, and lending practices. It gives you everything you need to know about how to protect your scores if they're high and improve them if they're not. The days of easy lending aren't likely to come back anytime soon. So now more than ever, knowing how to fix, improve, and protect your credit score is essential for successfully navigating your financial life.

10 Secrets To Better Mortgage Rates Banks Never Tell You:

The mortgage industry is not what it use to be. 100% stated income loans if you had a credit score of 620 or better are gone. Some unscrupulous Wall Street executives made sure they took the

# How To Raise Your Credit Score

mortgage industry to the edge and unfortunately part of it fell off. This has caused both record numbers of foreclosures and additional stress these families are facing.

Maybe some people could afford a home, but just not the $350,000 one. The mortgage industry has a responsibility to both educate home buyers and build lifetime relationships. We must look at the long-term goals of owning a home, rather than owning what we want now. Build yourself in the 'Best Borrower' so you can get the home that you have always wanted, it is really not that difficult. If you make your mortgage payment a struggle, it will only hurt you in the end.

There is something to be said about the years of 'buyer education' our parents went through to buy their first home. It created financial strength. Often times it took years to accumulate enough money to buy the American Dream. Imagine both the financial commitments and attention to credit that must have had? Did you know that the subprime mortgage industry is really less than 20 years old? It was only recently that the birth of the 'not so perfect' credit mortgage and 'now you need less than 20% down' mortgages were born

Ironically, it's these new ideas that have allowed many more people to own a home. The United States has recently achieved its highest percentage of home ownership in our history. Obviously

# How To Raise Your Credit Score

home ownership is great; however, it can show it's ugly face with foreclosures and all the stress it causes as well.

So we would like to offer you the '10 ways to be your best borrower in a changing mortgage world'. Everything in this world has fundamentals and building blocks that we can apply if we are to get the most out of them. This guidance will make you a stronger borrower and will get you better mortgage interest rates.

1) Pay your rent/mortgage on time with checks. Banks want to see consistent payments on your bills. None is more important than your current rent or mortgage. Even if their landlord lives next door, pay by a check. Days of a private Verification of Mortgage have gone away. This stability in payment shows a stronger borrower.
2) When building credit, pay on time and avoid high balances. We are looking at buying a home twelve months from now. Pay a little extra every month. Stay away from programs that say "18 months same as cash". Most likely these programs will give you a credit line for the amount of the unit you are purchasing. For example, that large screen TV for the big game. The line is maxed when you buy the unit. New credit opened and then it's maxed. This has many negative effects.
3) Stay in that car for a couple more months. Get in the home and then go after the car. This can really drive your score down.

## How To Raise Your Credit Score

4) Buy a home within your means. This will allow you to keep the home and get the home that they want when they can afford it. This benefits all of us.

5) For cash paying incomes - Deposit your money first! Many banks have 12 months bank statement programs. This can allow you to avoid stated income products and higher rates. We all love our extra part-time bartending job. Showing this income to a lender will help as well.

6) When paying down credit lines, keep them open. Don't pay them off. Credit lines that are paid off negatively affect credit

7) Educate yourself. Stay up in tune with mortgage industry trends. For example, right now a 40-year mortgage is better than an interest only or a 50-year program. The secondary market, which drives mortgage programs, and rates, looks negatively on 50 year and interest-only products. When this happens your rates become higher.

8) Look at the benefits of refinancing. Most lenders use these guidelines called Net Tangible Benefits. This is there to protect you as a borrower. Are you getting 10% cash out? Are you lowering their payment by 10%? Are you moving from an Adjustable Rate to a Fixed Rate? If there is no benefit, think again. This is probably not the lender for you.

9) Know what payment will affect your credit the most. Your home and your car can affect you the worse. It can take 12 months to repair this damage. Don't ever think one payment won't hurt.

# How To Raise Your Credit Score

10) Before you refinance, can you take out a Home Equity Line of Credit? Most HELOC's do not have a prepayment penalty. Take one out to repair the credit and pay off debts and then refinance. Over time a borrower will save more than the costs of the HELOC because their mortgage interest rates are lower. 40 to 100 points in your score can make a lot of difference to your rate.

If you know the 10 Secrets to obtaining your best mortgage terms before you buy a home, you definitely will save thousands of dollars.

In the United States, your credit score is everything. It is something that you should take care of. If you don't, getting a phone, cable or gas line hooked up to your home can be difficult to do.

There are also certain companies that take a look at your credit score first before they even hire you. Even if you are qualified to do the job, a low credit score can ruin it all for you. Your credit score is also analyzed by creditors, such as banks and credit card companies. Just try to imagine that you need to get a loan to start your own business, with a low or bad credit score, you have a lesser chance of getting that loan approved or you may get it approved but with high-interest rates.

The same thing goes when you apply for a credit card. Credit card companies or banks that issue credit cards will first take a look at

# How To Raise Your Credit Score

your credit score before they can get your application approved. A high credit score means that you have a greater chance of getting the best credit card deals with a lot of features and also with low-interest rates for your every purchase using a certain credit card.

Even if you are applying for a mortgage, a car loan and other kinds of loans, your credit score will play a very important role in it. This is why it is very important for you to have a high credit score and maintain it that way or increase it.

First of all, you have to understand what a credit score actually is.

A credit score will be a three digit number from 300 to 850. This number will represent a calculation of the likelihood of whether you will pay their bills or not. This means that if you have a high credit score, creditors will be sure that you a better credit risk than someone with a low credit score.

In the United States, FICO (or Fair Isaac Corporation) is the best-known credit score model in the country. They calculate your credit score using a formula developed by FICO. The system is used primarily by credit industries and consumer banking industries all across the country.

## Credit scores calculation factors

Credit scores are calculated using the following factors:

# How To Raise Your Credit Score

- Punctuality of payments

    This will be 35% of the calculation. If you pay your bills on time or before the due date, your credit score will tend to be higher.

- Capacity used

    This will amount to 30% of the calculation of your credit score. It will contain a ratio between the current revolving debts to total available revolving credit. If you use your credit card and if you don't use its entire credit limit, you will get a higher credit score.

- Length of credit history

    This will amount to 15% of the calculation of your credit score.

- Types of credit used

    This can affect 10% of your total credit score.

- Recent search for credit or the amount of credit obtained recently

    This will amount to 10% of the total calculation of your credit score.

Surprisingly, not many people know their credit score and often end up wondering why they got denied for their loan or credit card application. You can easily obtain a copy of your credit report by re uesting for it from the three major credit reporting agencies.

# How To Raise Your Credit Score

The law allows you to order a copy of your free credit score from each of the nationwide consumer reporting companies every 12 months. How can you find out what your credit score is?

Your credit score it is one of the most critical factors in your financial life. It determines if you will be approved for a loan or line of credit. A credit score is a mathematically calculated number developed by the Fair Isaac Corporation (FICO) that lenders use to rate potential customers in determining the likelihood that a customer will pay their bills on time. A credit score or credit rating is determined by using five main criteria as defined by MyFico.com: your payment history which accounts for 35% of your credit score, the amounts owed which accounts for 30% of your credit score, the length of your credit history which accounts for 15% of your credit score, new credit which accounts for 10% of your credit score, and the types of credit used which accounts for 10% of your credit score.

Payment history shows the history of how you paid your bills either on time or late but unfortunately does not show if your bills were paid before the due date. Amounts owed shows the total amount of credit you have available. If your balance is near the credit limit this may lower your credit score. The length of history indicates how long you have had credit. If your credit history is 2 years or less could lower your credit score. New credit indicates how many times you have applied for new credit. If you open two many new accounts in a short period of time this may lower your

## How To Raise Your Credit Score

credit score. The types of credit used indicate the types of accounts you have such as revolving or installment accounts. Revolving accounts are usually credit cards and installment accounts are usually mortgages, auto loans, etc.

The FICO credit score model ranges from 300-850 with 850 being an excellent score and 300 being the worst score. The higher the credit score the lower the interest rate you will receive for a loan or line of credit. Having a good credit score can save you thousands of dollars in interest over the life of the loan or line of credit. A good credit score is generally in the range of 660-749 but may vary from lender to lender.

The three major credit bureaus Experian, Equifax and TransUnion use the FICO credit score model. Equifax uses the Beacon credit score, Experian uses the Fair Isaac or Plus score and TransUnion uses the Empirica score. Each credit bureau subscribes to the Fair Isaac's FICO model of scoring and then integrates their own version of a consumer's FICO score. The Equifax Beacon score ranges from 340-820. The TransUnion Empirica score ranges from 150-934. The Fair Isaac or Plus score ranges from 330-830.

When applying for credit or a loan if all three credit scores are pulled, the middle score is generally the score used with the application, but according to the Fair Isaac Corporation, 75% of mortgage loan applications use the Fair Isaac or Plus score.

# How To Raise Your Credit Score

Your credit score varies from each bureau because each agency collects their own data from various sources and may collect different data for the same account. Your score can vary anywhere from 5-40 points between the three credit bureaus. Your credit score changes due to updates to your credit file which changes based on account activity such as balance changes or additions to your credit file (i.e. new accounts or deletion of older negative accounts more than 7 or 10 years old). As a result, you may see a difference in your score from one month to the next.

## Criteria Not Included in Calculation of Credit Score

The following criteria are not included in calculating your credit score:

1. If rent or you own a home
2. Income
3. Length of time at your current job
4. Length of time at your current address
5. Whether you've been denied credit

However, the above may be considered in approval for a loan in addition to using your credit score.

## 5 Things to Boost your Credit Score:

If you have a low credit score here are 5 things you can do to boost your credit score:

1. Stop using your credit cards and pay with cash.

# How To Raise Your Credit Score

2. Pay more than the monthly minimum. If you can't, it's time to cut spending.
3. Develop a plan to reduce your total debt.
4. Reduce your interest rates, but be careful of the fine print-- a credit card with 0% interest could cost you thousands in interest depending on how the credit card is structured.
5. Get a part-time job in addition to your full-time job or find ways to reduce expenses and use the extra money to pay down debt.

The major disadvantage of credit scoring is that it relies on information in your credit report which may contain errors. It is estimated that 75% of credit reports contain at least one error. That's why it is so important that you check your credit report at least once a year to ensure that all information is accurate and up to date.

If you plan on purchasing a large item such as a car, house or investment property, it is best to pull your credit yourself to see if any negative items appear so you can fix those issues before applying for a loan. The best way to understand your credit score is to do research and read the information that is provided when you order your credit report.

## What is Credit Score?

The FICO assessment is the report card for your whole record of loan repayment. The FICO assessment is for the most part

# How To Raise Your Credit Score

computed through a meter which ranges from 0 to 850. These diverse classifications or components which are considered at the season of ascertaining your FICO rating are installment history (35%), obligation and advance (30%), length of financial record (15%), new credit (10%) and sort of credit accounts utilized (10%). These elements are essential for getting a decent FICO rating. You can likewise think about the best tips to enhance your financial assessment.

## How is Credit Score Calculated?

Check the best factors that you generally need to recall for having the best FICO rating. These distinctive components are considered by the banks and the last FICO rating is figured on the outcomes.

### Installment History (35%)

It considers acknowledge records, for example, charge cards, credit extensions, retail chain accounts, portion advances, automobile advances, understudy advances, back organization accounts, home value advances and home loan advances.

Make installments on time
- It has positive effect
- Is the most crucial factor
- It represents 35% of your score

# How To Raise Your Credit Score

- It demonstrates whether you make installments on time, how frequently you miss installments
- Obligation and Loan (30%)

It considers and is totally in light of the whole sum you owe, the number and sorts of records you have. You should realize that, that the new credits with little installment history may drop your score.

- Pay off your advances
- Attempt to make online installment moreover
- It represents 30% of your score
- Lower your FICO assessment through high adjusts
- It computes aggregate sum versus the sum due
- what is FICO rating? How FICO assessment is ascertained
- Record (15%)

The record is the last factor that is constantly considered at the season of influencing the credit to report and furthermore computing your FICO rating. It checks the whole history of your credit ideal from the begin till the end.

- It represents 15% of your score
- Checks your whole record of loan repayment
- Considers your old record
- Additionally checks the dates of new records

# How To Raise Your Credit Score

- Endeavor to keep your record of loan repayment clear of any obligation
- Record Type (10%)

You should consider the numerous sorts of records that you by and large have. The kinds of advances have portion advances, home advances, and retail and Visas may enhance your score and know the best sort.

- Have more exchange lines dependably
- Endeavor to have numerous tradelines
- It represents 10% of your score
- All records ought to dependably be refreshed
- Comprises of portion advances, home advances, and retail and Visas
- Late Credit (10%)

The most recent sorts of updates or exchanges are likewise a vital factor to compute and enhance your FICO rating. Alongside the following biggest segment is the sum that you as of now owe.

- Have less new credits
- Consider asks
- It represents 10% of your score
- Your current credit is likewise essential
- Records which are over 20 years of age are used for credit

# How To Raise Your Credit Score

Everyone wants good credit score. A credit score is generally calculated through a meter which ranges from 0 to 850.

## What Damages Credit And How It Can Prevent

Banish these myths from the way you handle your credit! Your score will be as good as it can be when you know the truth about how these actions affect your credit score.

Damaging Myths:

Myth # 1:

**Closing inactive accounts will raise your score:**

This is a widely held belief, but it's false. Closing accounts, whether or not they have zero balances, whether or not they're inactive, will often lower your scores. Why? Because part of your credit score is based on the ratio of your credit card debt to your total available credit. If you close a zero-balance account with significant available credit, this ratio gets smaller. It's as simple as that.

On the other hand, you can also have too much of a good thing (too much available credit compared to your ability to pay). If you're concerned that this may be true in your case, then you can close zero-balance accounts that you don't need. If you plan to close more than one zero-balance account, wait a few months in between. Each closing will initially affect your score adversely, and it can take months for the scores to be adjusted upward.

# How To Raise Your Credit Score

Myth # 2:

**It doesn't matter what balance is on each card; it's the total that counts:**

Again, this is untrue. Another part of your score is calculated by looking at the debt to available credit ratio on each card individually. Ideally, keep this under 30% on every one of your cards. For example, if your credit line on a card is $2500, keep the balance below $750.

Pay your debt down instead of moving it around to other revolving accounts. Moving it around (for instance, moving balances to zero or low-interest credit cards) can lower your scores. With all the offers for low initial rates, many consumers are moving their credit card balances over and over again, trying to keep their accounts at the lower rates. If you're moving balances among accounts that you already have open, and if you can do it without going over 30% on each account, then this is okay. But if it means applying for a new account each time, don't do it. Each application will lower your score.

Myth # 3:

**More accounts and greater available credit always means a higher score:**

Not true. Don't open new accounts you don't need trying to increase your available credit. It can backfire. You need only four

# How To Raise Your Credit Score

open and active accounts to establish great credit scores. Apply for credit only as you truly need it.

Many folks fall for department store promotions. The offer to get 10 or 20% off if you open an account may look like a great deal, but the activity can be detrimental to your credit scores. Don't open accounts thinking it will raise your score, as it may not help at all. Have credit cards, but use them wisely. It is actually viewed that someone that has a good history of responsible credit use is a lower risk than someone with no credit cards at all. For the best score, ideally, you should have a mix of installment credit (cars, furniture, etc) along with credit cards and mortgages.

Myth # 4:

**Your credit reports are complete and accurate, even if you never make sure of it:**

If you have ever had a collection account, judgment or tax lien, don't assume that the creditor, collection agency or taxing body will report the resolution to all three bureaus. That goes for erroneous reporting you find on your report too. Don't assume that because you paid off a collection, judgment, or lien that it is immediately reported to the bureaus. Even when you close an account, it is often not efficiently reported as such to all bureaus. It is not uncommon to see such activity reported to just one bureau, even when the adverse account was being reported on your credit report by two or all three bureaus.

# How To Raise Your Credit Score

Unfortunately, agencies and creditors are quick to report you when you owe them money or have made a recent mistake, but they can be very slow to report the final resolution to that account when you have paid them. This problem is magnified when there has been a bankruptcy. Accounts that have been involved in a bankruptcy may have been moved between the creditors and various collection agencies long before the filing for bankruptcy protection. The creditor is reporting the account as delinquent and is likely reported it as a charge-off.

But the creditor has also sold the account to a collection agency, hoping to get a small percentage of their loss back if the agency can collect anything. This goes for credit cards, department store accounts and even installment loans like auto loans. The account is sold back and forth between creditors and agencies.

The problem is that after one file for bankruptcy protection, and after the time has passed that it takes to successfully bankrupt the debts, the accounts may be sold multiple times. In addition, it is not uncommon to see an account go to the collection after it has been discharged in a bankruptcy. You are thinking that you have a fresh start to rebuild your credit after the bankruptcy, yet there may be new collection accounts dated after the discharge which has a huge impact on your already damaged credit scores.

What's the remedy? Watch your credit reports like a hawk! No one else cares nearly as much as you do about making sure they're

# How To Raise Your Credit Score

accurate. You have to follow up with each individual bureau and supply them with copies of your discharge and lists of creditors to ensure that everything is reflected accurately on your overall credit report. It can take years to see a rise in your credit scores if you don't follow through with this. It is your responsibility to watch any such activity and make sure that all three bureaus have the most recent and accurate information possible. You can write and/or file online disputes with each individual bureau and supply copies of paid receipts and any correspondence you may have to ensure that your record is recent and correct.

# Chapter 2: Why Your Credit Score Matters

In recent years, a simple three-digit number has become critical to your financial life. This number, known as a credit score, is designed to predict the possibility that you won't pay your bills. Credit scores are handy for lenders, but they can have enormous repercussions for your wallet, your future, and your peace of mind.

Your FICO or credit score is an overall evaluation of your financial health that helps lenders determine your creditworthiness. Credit scores affect whether you can get credit and what you pay for credit cards, auto loans, mortgages and other types of credit. Higher credit scores mean you are more likely to be approved for most kinds of credit and pay a lower interest rate for that credit.

Your credit score can come between you and many things in life. Since a FICO score is the excepted standard for many companies, a low score will mean you have to pay higher interest rates, if you can get a loan at all. It can also mean that you will have to pay higher deposits for utilities such as telephone, electricity, cellular phone plans and many other services. While this may not seem fair to most consumers, it is done by companies to determine whether or not they can rely on you to pay your bills on time.

## How To Raise Your Credit Score

Typically, those with a lower credit score have issues with paying their debts or paying them on time. This indicates to companies and banks that the person is probably a high-risk case and if they do decide to approve the loan or service, they must protect themselves from that risk by charging more. It is an excepted practice that can restrict or impede the lives of many people.

Your credit score is a valuable asset for many reasons. A very good score allows you to obtain credit more easily and at lower interest rates. But a high credit score can also help you qualify for a cell phone, avoid or reduce a deposit paid for utilities for your home or apartment, and get lower insurance premiums. Your credit score may also be used by potential employers and landlords as a screening tool. Your credit score is very valuable, and you should treat it like the asset it is and always work on improving it.

Three-quarters of all lenders use FICO scores when considering requests for loans or credit. To enhance your chances of being approved for any type of credit and get the best interest rates, your score should be 720 or higher.

Lenders look at your credit scores all the time. They look at your scores when deciding, for example, to extend credit to you, or whether to change your interest rate or credit limit on an existing credit card or to send you an offer through the mail. Having good credit scores makes your financial transactions much easier and can save you money on lower interest rates, lower insurance

# How To Raise Your Credit Score

premiums, and reduced deposits or down payments. That's why your credit score is a vital part of your financial health.

## How Your Credit Score Affects You

If your credit score is high enough, you'll qualify for a lender's best rates and terms. Your mailbox will be stuffed with low-rate offers from credit card issuers, and mortgage lenders will fight for your business. You'll get great deals on auto financing if you need a car, home loans if you want to buy or improve a house, and small business loans if you decide to start a new venture. If your score is low or nonexistent, however, you'll enter a no-man's land where mainstream credit is all but impossible to come by. If you find someone to lend you money, you'll pay high rates and fat fees for the privilege. A bad or even mediocre credit score can easily cost you tens of thousands and even hundreds of thousands of dollars in your lifetime. You don't even have to have tons of credit problems to pay a price. Sometimes all it takes is a single missed payment to knock more than 100 points off your credit score and put you in a lender's high-risk category. That would be scary enough if we were just talking about loans. But landlords and insurance companies also use credit scores to evaluate applicants. A good score can win you cheaper premiums and better apartments; a bad score can make insurance more expensive and a place to live hard to find.

# How To Raise Your Credit Score

Yet too many people know far too little about credit scores and how they work. Here's just a sample of the kinds of emails and letters I get every day from people puzzling over their credit:

"I just closed all of my credit card accounts trying to improve my credit.

Now I hear that closing accounts can actually hurt my score. How can I recover from this? Should I try to reopen accounts so that I can have a higher amount of available credit?" Hallie in Shreveport, LA"

*I joined a credit-counseling program because I was in way over my head. But my wife and I plan on buying a house within the next three*

years, and she has expressed concern that my participation in this debt management program could hurt my credit score. What should I do to help my overall chances with the mortgage process and get the best rate possible?" Paul in Lodi, NJ

What these readers sense, and what credit experts know, is that ignorance about your credit score can cost you. Sometimes people with great scores get offered lousy loan deals but don't realize they can qualify for better terms. More often, people with bad or mediocre credit get approved for loans but don't realize the high price they're paying.

# HOW TO RAISE YOUR CREDIT SCORE

What It Costs Long Term to Have a Poor or Mediocre Credit Score
If you need an example of exactly how much a credit score can matter, let's examine how these numbers affect two friends, Emily and Karen. Both women got their first credit card in college and carried an $8,000 balance on average over the years. (Carrying a balance isn't smart financially, but unfortunately, it's an ingrained habit with many credit card users.) Emily and Karen also bought new cars after graduation, financing their purchases with $20,000 auto loans. Every seven years, they replaced their existing cars with new ones until they bought their last vehicles at age 70. Each brought her first home with $350,000 mortgages at age 30 and then moved up to a larger house with $450,000 mortgages after turning 40.

Neither has ever suffered the embarrassment of being rejected for a loan or turned down for a credit card. But here the similarities end. Emily was always careful to pay her bills on time, all the time, and typically paid more than the minimum balance owed. Lenders responded to her responsible use of credit by offering her more credit cards at good rates and terms. They also tended to increase her credit limits regularly. That allowed Emily to spread her credit card balance across several cards. All these factors helped give Emily an excellent credit score. Whenever a lender tried to raise her interest rate, she would politely threaten to transfer her balance to another card. As a result, Emily's average interest rate on her cards was 9.9 percent. Karen, by contrast, didn't always pay on

## How To Raise Your Credit Score

time, frequently paid only the minimum due and tended to max out the cards that she had. That made lenders reluctant to increase her credit limits or offer her new cards. Although the two women owed the same amount on average, Karen tended to carry larger balances on fewer cards. All these factors hurt Karen's credit—not enough to prevent her from getting loans, but enough for lenders to charge her more. Karen had much less negotiating power when it came to interest rates. Her average interest rate on her credit cards was 19.9 percent.

Emily's careful credit use paid off with her first car loan. She got the best available rate, and she continued to do so every time she bought a new car until her last purchase at age 70. Thanks to her lower credit score, Karen's rate was three percentage points higher.

Karen's total lifetime penalty for less-than-stellar credit? More than $190,000.

If anything, these examples underestimate the true financial cost of mediocre credit:

- The interest rates in the examples are relatively low in historical terms. Higher prevailing interest rates would increase the penalty that Karen pays.
- Karen probably paid insurance premiums that were 20 percent to 30 percent higher than Emily's and she might have had more trouble finding an apartment, all because of her credit.

## How To Raise Your Credit Score

- The examples don't count "opportunity cost"—what Karen could have achieved financially if she weren't paying so much more interest.

Because more of Karen's paycheck went to lenders, she had less money available for other goals: vacations, a second home, college educations for her kids, and retirement. In fact, if Karen had been able to invest the extra money she paid in interest instead of sending it to banks and credit card companies, her savings might have grown by a whopping $2 million by the time she was 70. With so much less disposable income and financial security, you wouldn't be surprised if Karen also experienced more anxiety about money. Financial problems can take their toll in innumerable ways, from stress-related illnesses to marital problems and divorce.

# Chapter 3: How Credit Scoring Works

Understanding how credit scores work is the first step in maximizing or fixing damaged credit either with the help of a credit repair firm or on your own. First, you need to know that the higher your credit score the better whether you are looking for a new credit card, shopping for a mortgage or trying to buy a new or used vehicle. The higher your score the better risk you are considered when applying for any amount of credit. Knowing what goes into the calculation of your credit score and what can affect it either positively or negatively can help you make the proper moves to maximize your score at all times.

Here are some factors to help you understand how credit scores work. FICO (Fair Isaac Corporation) scores are a compilation of scores from the three credit reporting agencies Experian, TransUnion and Equifax. Each of the credit reporting companies has their own version based on different algorithms so the scores will vary. In addition not all companies that report their accounts report to all three agencies. Equifax has what is called a BEACON score, TransUnion has the EMPIRE score and Experian uses a combination FICO risk analysis score. Recently the three agencies have cooked up a combined score that very few people use called the VantageScore and are available from Experian's website. You

# How To Raise Your Credit Score

can no longer get the real Experian score which can cause problems when getting a mortgage loan as you will no longer be able to maximize your middle score if Experian was your middle score.

Thirty-five percent (35%) of your credit score is based on how often you pay your bills on time. Another thirty percent (30%) is based on how much debt you have in relation to how much credit you have - in other words your debt to credit ratio. Fifteen percent (15%) is based on the length of your credit history. If you have several accounts open longer than ten years you will get more points than having several new accounts. Ten percent (10%) is based on your mix of credit - credit cards, mortgage, auto loan, revolving credit lines and installment credit lines. A good mix will give you more points as it shows you have a good sense of how to take care of your credit. New credit accounts for only ten percent (10%) of your score.

Some of the things in learning how credit scores work are what is left out when calculating your scores. Here is a list of what is not taken into account - your age, sex, or race. In addition how long you have been at your current job or how many jobs you have had is not looked at. Your income, marital status, number of children, or level of education are also not considered. You may wonder if the number of times you have been turned down for credit will affect your scores - it doesn't. Owning or renting your home, how

# How To Raise Your Credit Score

long you have been at your current address or any criminal record is also not considered when calculating your credit scores.

Like it or not you are judged by a number and not your situation when it comes to getting a loan. Your credit score can make you or break you. It is no secret that having a good credit score will increase your chances of obtaining a new loan or credit card but many people do not realize this value until it is too late. It is time to learn how credit scores work.

There are quite a number of factors that come into play when figuring out a credit score. An end result is a number that can range between 300 and 850. This is on an increasing scale so the higher the number, the better credit rating you have.

It is possible to have a credit score of 850 but it is not easy. All payments have to be on time, all payments need to be for the full amounts, and how long it takes to pay off certain loans or debts is also considered. However, you do not need an 850 credit score just to have what is considered as "good credit". A credit score of about 650 to 700 and above is usually considered a good credit score. If you want to qualify for things such as prime rates on mortgage loans then you should shoot for about 680 and above.

When determining how credit scores work, we need to look at payment history, outstanding debts, inquiries, and the length of your credit history. The main factors are your outstanding debts and your payment history. These will weight heavily when

# How To Raise Your Credit Score

determining your credit score. Before a lender decides to give you money they want to see if you are typically on time for your payments. The more often you are late, the less they want to lend you money. If your outstanding debts are very high, they might not want to lend you money for fear that you will not be able to pay all your debts back (mainly theirs).

Lenders depend on credit scores every day to decide whether or not a loan applicant should be approved. Using the credit score is an efficient way to make this decision due to the high volume of requests lenders receive each day. A simple query will let them know if you are a potentially good or bad client. While lenders may have other criteria for approving a loan, the credit score is a quick way to weed out those whose credit history is less than desirable.

If you find yourself in the latter category then you should start working on improving your credit score immediately. Since payment history plays a large role in calculating your credit score you should begin paying all current bills on time. The second largest piece is your outstanding debts. Get your own credit report for yourself and see how much money you owe to certain companies. Work on paying these off immediately. Call these companies and see if you can work out a deal where the payments are less per month. Some collectors will settle for a lesser amount if you pay in full. Knowing how credit scores work is the first step to having a more financially stable life.

# How To Raise Your Credit Score

# Chapter 4: Improving Your Score—The Right Way 5

There might be different factors for your failure to repay a loan on time. Whatever be the reason, if someone has not repaid a loan on time, it will surely affect his credit record and his rating will come down significantly. With the lowering of credit rating, the chances for getting a loan in future will also be reduced. Therefore, you should always try to pay back your loan on time and keep your credit record unaffected. However, if you have already got a poor record, you should learn how to improve credit score.

If you want to get your record repaired, you need to be careful about the expenses you are making. Be more calculative about the money that you are spending and try to save as much as possible. Use the saved money in repaying the old debts and getting your score repaired. When you have a huge amount of outstanding, you should know how to improve credit score fast by manipulating your money.

Someone who is worried about his low score and wants to know how to improve the score easily should stop the use of credit cards at once. In most of the cases, people incur huge debts after credit card shopping. So, it is always advisable to stop using such cards when you want to get your ratings repaired. Even if you use a card,

# How To Raise Your Credit Score

you should make sure to do proper calculations before making any transaction with it.

Student's credit cards are one of the most prominent causes of getting bad credits. If this is the same in your case and you want to know how to improve your score quickly, you should get the student card of your child blocked immediately. Whether someone has the bad record or not, it is never advisable to allow your child use a card as he/she does not have any idea regarding the right use of this card.

When you want to know how to improve your score, you can always take the assistance of financial experts, who can offer proper consultation against some charges. Debt settlement and debt consolidation are some of the most important ways of getting your score improved. By taking these services, you can get your loan repaid in a few installments. Yet, before taking any of these services, you should always spend some time to note the pros and cons of each of the services.

If like many of us, your credit score is less than perfect, there are several ways you can improve it. Now you could hire a credit repair company to help you with this, but I suggest you save your money. Realistically, there is not much they can do for you that you can't do for yourself if you just know how. Sure, they'll charge you lots of money and 2 years and $2000 later your score won't

# How To Raise Your Credit Score

look any better than if you had saved yourself the $2000 and done the work yourself.

## Improve your payment history

1. Start making our payments on time and avoid late payments at all costs.
2. Clear up past bills quickly paying off high-interest bills first. This saves you money in interest fees and reduces your total debt and time needed to pay off debts.
3. Contact your creditors to see if a lower, more manageable payment can be arranged.
4. Ask if charge-offs can be removed from your record and accounts reopened.
5. See if creditors will erase late payment entries when you start paying on time.

## Decrease outstanding debts

1. Pay debts that have higher interest rates first.
2. Keep balances low and keep revolving debt such as credit cards to 30% of available credit.
3. Never close old unused accounts quickly. This can have a negative effect on your score.

# How To Raise Your Credit Score

4. Close accounts slowly and check your credit report to be sure the closed accounts are listed as closed by consumer.

## Get a better history

If your credit history is new, do not open a lot of accounts quickly. Creditors perceive this as a sign that you can not manage your credit.

## Manage credit effectively

1. Don't open a new account with a large credit limit but rather confine your account at a medium limit.
2. Do not open too many accounts at once.
3. Consider credit payments when making your budget.
4. Do not apply for too many accounts at once since these inquiries can negatively affect your score.

## Keep a proper mix of the right results

1. Too many installment loans reduce your score since the payments remain the same over time.
2. A combo of credit cards and installment loans is it ideal mix. However, manage the cards effectively, staying within the 30% of available credit range. Pay these balances quickly.

# HOW TO RAISE YOUR CREDIT SCORE

3. Open a savings account. This action will encourage your creditors to think you are saving money to pay down your debts.
1. Finally, remember to make your payments on time and monitor your credit report. Remove any errors from this report.

# Chapter 5: Coping With A Credit Crisis

We are in a recession, and regardless of how many news ebooks we read of people claiming that the recession is nearly over, the story in people's homes are far from it. Some are not only worried about paying their next mortgage or rent payment but worried about where the food will come from to put on the tables, it is fair to say we have not seen a situation like this for many years, however, what can we do to survive?

The most important thing that must be done is to ensure you talk about your situation to those who can help and advice you on what you can do to keep your head above the water. Losing a job could mean a temporary loss of income; in this case, keeping your ears to the ground and eyes open for any job opportunity could be all that is required to put you back into financial security which enables you to afford to live. For those where there simply are no jobs available at this time, if you owe money to creditors, including your mortgage, you need to ensure you do not bury your head in the sand and ignore the situation, but talk to the companies involved and explain the situation. Creditors can reduce payments and mortgage companies can offer a payment break, they cannot, however, offer these if they are not aware that there is a problem.

# How To Raise Your Credit Score

It is surprising how many people are not aware of what they are paying out each month, this includes how much they pay on household bills as well as keeping an eye on what they are spending on shopping.

Working out a budget based on what payments go out each month can help tremendously when it comes to staying in control of your finances. Before the credit crunch had an effect, it was all too easy to spend money and not take note of what we were spending, so working out how much needs to be paid out each month as well as creating a budget which keeps us from overspending on things that are not necessary could help us see the bigger picture and know exactly what we need as priority payments each month.

It would also be fair to say that most of us do not shop around for the cheapest options when it comes to gas, electricity, telephone companies and the likes. We are used to sticking with the same company for years and do not keep an eye on what their competitors are doing as well as whether or not they are a cheaper option which could save us money over the year. By looking at other companies rates, we could save ourselves some money.

As well as looking at what you are spending, check out what benefits you may qualify for in your situation. Benefits such as housing benefits, job seekers allowance, help with health costs and educational costs can all make a massive difference when it comes to coping with a reduced income.

# How To Raise Your Credit Score

Suffering from the credit crunch and struggling to make ends meet during this time of this financial crisis leaves no room for pride, so if it means accepting help from benefits available, it is most certainly an option to take advantage of. It is all too easy to look around to borrow money to pay off creditors at a time like this, however, instead of borrowing more money, work out how much you can realistically afford to repay each of your creditors and offer them that amount until your situation improves. This helps you to pay off your debt rather than getting you further into debt.

Don't be afraid to ask for help, thousands of people are in the same situation as you and are doing whatever it takes in order to cope with living in the current economy and also by getting help, you are reducing the impact and stress that the situation is having in the home and your relationships.

# Chapter 6: Rebuilding Your Score After a Credit Disaster

Getting on the road to improvement with your credit seems like a battle, but the fact is it took many years to screw up your credit and it is going to take years to get back to a good standing. Here are some methods to help you on your way. If you are looking to start rebuilding your credit, one of the first things you should do is get a copy of your credit report. You want to review it not only to see where you are but also check for any potential errors. If there are errors more than likely they are hurting your score and if removed could give you an initial boost.

Moving on, the most important commitment you must make is to never pay your bills late. Your payment history makes up the largest portion of your credit score and paying late will kill your chances for improvement. A monthly budget is a great tool to make sure you have the money to pay your bills and you do it on time. Also, if you not current with any of your accounts you must do anything you can to get current.

The next step is to develop a plan to reduce the amount of debt you have. Your debt to credit ratio is the next largest portion of your credit score and carry high debt will hold you back. From here on out, you must not spend on your credit cards and use your budget to find money to apply to your debt. If you want a jump start, you should have a sale on eBay to sell everything that is not bolted down or even get a second job.

So what happens if you had to file for bankruptcy or have a lot of negative marks on your credit report? Some people get discouraged after being turned down for credit or loans and just give up. Other people who know how the credit system works can start building their credit back up. How fast you can recover from your mistakes depends on you and what you do right away. Understanding how the system works gives you the advantage of time. When you're given a fresh start, you can put the past behind you right away. Credit scoring formulas are more concerned with what you've done recently than what has happened in the past, so it's important to get started off right. Rebuilding your score will still take some time, but if done right, you could significantly boost your score within a couple years. If it's been about seven years since your last negative mark (or up to ten years for a Chapter 7 bankruptcy), your credit score could be above average.

## Part 1: Credit Report Repair

People who have had credit problems are sometimes afraid to look at their credit report knowing they won't like what they will see. You might find out that not every little problem was reported in the first place, or you could find that everything was. It is important that you look at your report so that you know what you have to do

## How To Raise Your Credit Score

to help clean it up. For example, you could be the victim of a shady collection agency that has illegally "re-aged" a bad debt. This is when they take an older bad debt and try to make it look more recent than it really is to the credit bureaus. You should know that there are steps to help you clean up your report, and fight back against illegal tactics.

Check Your Report For Serious Errors - As mentioned, you should first get copies of your credit report from the three different agencies. It is important to note that you should get three separate reports, not the 3-in-1 or tri-merged reports, which don't contain all of the information you would get from the three separate reports. Things that you should look for are:

Delinquencies that are older than seven years or accounts listed as delinquent that don't include the date of delinquency Bankruptcies that are older than 10 years or that aren't listed in the specific chapter Judgements or paid liens older than seven years, paid-off debts listed as unpaid

Accounts that were wiped up by a bankruptcy filing still listed as "past due" instead of as "included in bankruptcy"

- ❖ More than one collection account for the same debt
- ❖ Collection accounts that don't show the date that the original account went delinquent
- ❖ Any accounts, delinquencies, collections, etc., that aren't yours

# How To Raise Your Credit Score

- When you do decide to dispute any errors with the agency, make sure you keep records of it in case you run into any problems.

## Know Your Rights

The rights that you have under the Fair Credit Reporting Act are:

1) The right to have your dispute investigated
2) The right to have erroneous information corrected
3) The right to a written response
4) The right to have a statement included in your file
5) The right to sue.

## Organize Your Attack:

If you have found any errors on your report, you will want to gather any evidence you have to dispute them and notify the credit bureaus. You should then follow up with the credit bureaus with a certified letter so that you get a return receipt. This will make sure to get their attention that there is an error and any failure to act would be a violation of the Fair Credit Reporting Act and grounds for a lawsuit. Usually, the credit bureaus will make the corrections. However, you should still monitor your credit reports to make sure the same error(s) doesn't come up again in the future. This is why it is important to keep records of everything and could help you get it removed more quickly in the future. If the credit bureau is still stating that there is no error, you could always try hiring a lawyer.

# How To Raise Your Credit Score

Sometimes a letter from them will be enough to get it fixed, otherwise, there is always the option of a lawsuit. If you need a referral for an attorney.

Unpaid Debts And Collections:

When it comes to collections, another part of the Fair Debt Collection Practices Act is that you have the right to have a collection account "validated." This means that the collector must prove that the debt is your responsibility and that they have the right to collect it from you. They also have to stop all collection activity until the provide evidence to you. If they are unable to do this, they must cease active collections and stop reporting the debt to the credit bureaus. It is important to note that this only applies to the collection agencies, not the original creditor. To validate a debt, the collector needs to get documentation from the original creditor to prove that you do owe the money. A lot of times, collectors don't have the documentation needed, as some debts have been transferred from different agencies. This process could help get rid of any accounts that truly don't belong to you or also get rid of some that actually do.

Statutes Of Limitations:

Credit bureaus or only allowed a limited time to report negative information, 7 to 10 years. The statute of limitations curbs the amount of time a creditor can sue you for a debt. Statutes of limitations can vary by state and the type of debt involved. Usually, it depends on the state that you live in, but not always. By making a payment on a bad debt, you can sometimes restart a previously expired statute of limitations in some states. If you have a debt that is still within the statute and a collector is not actively pursuing it, it may be best just to leave it alone and hope it goes off your credit report in a few years. By looking into it, you could catch the collectors attention and could end up affecting your score. If it is past statute, you would be OK looking into the bad debt in more detail.

Should You Pay Old Debts?

You legally owe a bad debt until its paid, settled, or erased in a bankruptcy. Some people wrongly assume that they are no longer responsible when a creditor charges off the debt. Charging off a debt is just an accounting term to account for it. Even if the bad debt falls off your credit report after seven years, it is still your responsibility. A creditor might not be able to report a debt, but they can still actively pursue it.

A Couple More Things To Remember:

Although you might have good intentions on paying off a bad debt, sometimes it can actually hurt your score by making it look more recent since credit formulas place more weight on recent items. Sometimes just contacting an old creditor can leave you open to a lawsuit because some states have provisions that allow a statute of limitation to be extended if you make a payment or simply just acknowledge that you owe it. If you ever co-signed a loan for

## How To Raise Your Credit Score

someone else, any delinquencies, charge-offs, or collections for that loan will be reported on your credit report as well.

## Part 2: Adding Positive Information To Your File

Try To Get Positive Accounts Reported - When you're trying to rebuild your credit, it can be upsetting if one or more of the good accounts that you pay on time on doesn't show up in all of your reports. Some creditors might not even bother to report to the credit bureaus. Subprime lenders are guilty of doing this out of fear that if they do, their competitors will come in to try to take business away from them. You can't force a creditor to report, but it doesn't hurt to ask.

Become An Authorized User Of A Credit Card :

You are going to need someone with a good credit score and their permission. By being added to someone else's credit card account that has a good credit history can give your report a quick boost. Also, if you are an authorized user (not joint) you're not liable for any debt the account holder may run up.

Get Credit Or Charge Cards If You Don't Have Any:

You may be fearful of this idea if you are just recovering from bad debt, but you need to have a credit or charge card to start rebuilding your score. You can apply for a secured card that has a limit equal to the deposit that you make. Bankrate.com has a great

# How To Raise Your Credit Score

section on secured cards. Even though some financial experts warn against them, department store or gas cards may be the easiest unsecured cards to get after a credit disaster.

## Get An Installment Loan:

This could be a personal loan or an auto loan. You might have higher rates than what you would like, but this is to be expected after a negative credit report. Get A Cosigner - If you can't get a loan by yourself, you may need someone to cosign a loan with you. Just keep in mind that if you are unable to pay the loan, you are making the cosigner pay the price as well.

## Part 3: Use Your Credit Well

This part is pretty straightforward without needing much explanation. You should learn to pay your bills on time, use only the credit you have, keep your balances low, and don't apply for several lines of credit-especially in a short amount of time.

# Chapter 7: Identity Theft and Your Credit

You have most likely heard everything there is to know about identity theft and how it can destroy your credit. But what many people do not realize is that there are ways to overcome this type of crime and regain good standing with their credit. This is done by using professional credit repair services.

By now you most likely know how to prevent identity theft. Still, despite all efforts, thieves continue to come up with different ways to steal the identity of someone who has good credit. With each preventative method that is discovered, the ID thieves come up with a new approach to carry out their nefarious plans.

If you find out that you have been the victim of identity theft, you should get copies of your credit reports right away. You can see what damage has been done. You should also inform them that you have been the victim of this crime so that they can flag your accounts. This will prevent any new accounts from being opened in your name. This can be a hassle for you but will stop any further activity from occurring.

You will then need to file an affidavit stating that the debt accrued due to the theft is not from you. You will have to sign the affidavit, have it notarized and then send it to the credit bureau. You may have to do this on more than one account. In some cases, the lender will want an affidavit with a signature guarantee, which is a little bit more reliable than just a notary. You can usually get this service at your local bank. Some people report that they have a difficult time removing items that are not theirs from their credit reports and would rather hire a company to do this. You can use a credit repair service to remove errant items from your credit reports, although you will still have to sign some forms. If you have a difficult time reading a credit report, you might also want to consider using a service for this matter. It may be more effective than trying to perform this task yourself as it can end up costing you a great deal of time and at times can also be very frustrating.

Identity theft can really wreck your credit, but it does not have to. By using preventative measures, taking stock of your credit and using a credit rewind service, you can get your credit back to where it was before the ID thieves struck.

In this day and age, one of the most common types of crimes being committed the world over is identity theft. Therefore, it is important that you protect yourself against this type of crime. Moreover, you need to know what you must do if you find that you have become a victim. Through this ebook, you are provided information about how stolen identification can impact your credit score. You are also provided with information about what you

# How To Raise Your Credit Score

need to do in order to deal with your credit score after you have been a victim.

As an aside, you need to understand fully how crucial your credit standing is when it comes to being able to get a loan - or even a credit card. The fact is that a financial institution considering extending to you a loan of any type will first look at your score. If it does not meet a minimum level, these lenders will look no further. You also need to understand that many other businesses look at them as well before they will do business with you. This includes insurance companies and even some employers.

One of the insidious effects of being the victim of identity theft is the fact that this type of crime can do serious damage to your credit report and to your financial situation in general. Indeed, you very well may see your good rating plummet into the poor range in no time at all if you are the victim.

Therefore, when you have experienced this, you need to contact the three major reporting agencies to advise them of the situation. These reporting agencies will then put what is known as a fraud alert on your credit report. Through the placement of a fraud alert, you will be able to prevent further harm and damage to your personal financial reports.

Keep in mind that the work to correct your it is not concluded with the placement of a fraud alert. You must file an appropriate affidavit with the credit reporting agency (actually with all three reporting agencies) advising them in detail of the situation and that there is erroneous data on your report that needs to be changed and corrected.

# Chapter 8: Fixing Your Credit Score Fast

Having a poor credit score can not only negatively affect you financially - it can lead to lost job opportunities, rejected applications for tenancies and other seriously debilitating problems. If you have a credit score that could use a bit more than a simple boost, then you know exactly how it seems to follow you wherever you go. If you're sick and tired of always being refused for a credit card or paying more in interest rates just because you have poor credit, then it's time to use these fast fixes for your credit score - and get back on track right away:

1. Stop throwing your money at debts like your mortgage and student loan; instead, start focusing on paying off your credit card bills and any personal loans that you may have, as these kinds of debts drastically affect your credit score more than the other debts. While you may want to own your home faster or get rid of that student loan sooner, it's important to realize that this won't do much for your score. Yet when it comes to that one single credit card balance, you can really skyrocket your score just by throwing your money at it. When it comes to debt, it really pays to have the right ones taken care of first.

2. Don't spend more on your plastic than what you can pay. Credit reporting agencies frown on people who aren't able to

## How To Raise Your Credit Score

live within their means, which a balance on your credit card indicates. Create a household budget that sticks to your income, and make sure you don't over-exceed what you make by using your credit cards to fund that shopping spree.

3. Know your limits. It's a simple move that can save you big in the long run. Why is this, you ask? Simple: if you spend over your limit, not only will credit reporting agencies give you a black mark on your report - you'll end up having to pay some pretty hefty fees! This money is better spent paying off the principal of your debt, not some outrageous fees that go straight into a banker's pocket. Additionally, make sure that credit reporting agencies have your limits correct - often your credit score can be lowered unfairly if an agency has the wrong information. Call them on it and get your report updated for an instant boost.

4. Don't close any old credit card accounts that you might have. Your credit score is determined by the amount of credit versus debt that you have; therefore, the more credit you have (without balances, that is) the higher your credit score will be. This shows credit reporting agencies that you are trustworthy enough for lenders without living beyond your means.

5. Ask for a goodwill adjustment, where a happy lender might just erase a late payment from your credit score if you've been displaying good credit behavior. Wait for a year after making payments on time to request this, and you'll be seeing an improved score in no time!

# How To Raise Your Credit Score

Having a poor credit history does not necessarily mean it's the end of your future finance eligibility. Follow this guide and be proactive in the repair of your credit rating, and you will soon see fruits of your efforts.

The best way on how to improve credit score quickly if you have a bad credit record is to perform self-credit repair! Self-credit repair is a procedure where you argue unfavorable items on your credit report with the three main credit bureaus. This will involve sending argument letters to the three credit agencies to fix your credit score.

When these letters are received by the three credit agencies, they will try to examine your argument with your lender who is reporting about the negative items on your credit report. They will have 30 days to react and if they fail to give supporting evidence within the time given, the negative items will be removed from your credit report.

This is actually a simple process to fix your credit score. If you have ever been turned down for a loan or insurance that you wanted, you know that it does not sound right to you. In most cases, there may be some items that are reporting incorrectly on your credit report and you should start investigating and do a credit repair yourself in a reasonable time frame.

# How To Raise Your Credit Score

## How to Fix Your Credit Yourself

The most important thing you need to do right away is to obtain a complete history of your credit report to understand what has been going on in the past. Look closely to locate each item that could cause a red flag or lower your FICO scores on your credit report.

## What am I looking for precisely?

While looking over your credit information you want to first locate any discrepancy. Mistakes on your information are accounts that contain information that is not correct. It might be something regarding behind payment being recorded and you know you were never late for this payment. Another area you may also want to look at to fix your credit score is any over-limit items that are reported incorrectly and the credit bureaus assume that you are consistent in excess of your credit limit.

In addition, check for disparaging information such as delayed payments, charged off accounts, sets, rulings and economic failure. All of these will drag your credit score down ⬜uick.

## What Steps Should I perform to Correct These Accounts?

This is a crucial step on how to improve credit score. First, create a list of these accounts so they are separated from your fine accounts. Make sure that you position these accounts so that the oldest accounts are listed first and the latest accounts are listed last.

# How To Raise Your Credit Score

Then, you will need to issue credit argument correspondence letters to the first two accounts for each credit agency that is reporting the unfavorable information on this account. This is essential since there are three agencies and they all report in a different method so you want to make sure that you are not transferring an argument letter to an agency that is not reporting wrongfully about you!

## What should go on a Credit Argument Correspondence Letter and Why I am Writing It?

This correspondence is essentially telling the agencies that you do not have the same opinion with the information they are reporting on your credit report. The credit argument letter you are writing should contain your account number, name, address and social security number.

## How Will a Correspondence Assist Me to Repair My Credit?

Once your correspondence is received, the credit agencies, under Federal Law, have to examine this information with the original lender. If the original lender does not or will not give evidence of the information, then the agencies will have to eliminate the negative item from your report. Once the negative item on your credit report is detached, your scores will increase and your credit

# How To Raise Your Credit Score

will be repaired a little. In some occasions, your score may jump up 20 to 50 points!

This method of how to raise your credit score may vary depends on each individual situation and the nature of the negative item you originally have. Practicing on different available tools is very often the key to successfully fix your credit score.

# Chapter 9: Insurance and Your Credit Score

Many years ago your credit score didn't have an impact on your auto insurance premiums. Now however, it actually means how you live your life! And yes, this includes how much you pay for auto insurance. When you apply for auto insurance, the first thing the insurance companies do, after you complete their application, is run your credit. If your credit is bad to really poor, your premiums will be anywhere from $100.00 to $500.00 per year higher than someone who has a very high credit score.

Your premiums are based on first: your credit, second: your driving record. You would really think that a persons driving record would be more important. Most insurance companies however don't look at it that way. If your credit is bad, not only are your premiums higher, but some of the larger insurance companies won't even touch you. Then you are forced to go through the sub-prime insurance companies. These companies are not only higher in premiums, they also want a very large down payment. The monthly payments are also very high.

The problem is that when you have to pay such high premiums for having a bad credit score, you are spending money that could go to correcting your credit problems. Keeping your credit history clean

## How To Raise Your Credit Score

and your credit score high is very very important to ensure that your automobile insurance premiums stay low. Even people who are affected by a low score through no fault of their own, for example; laid off of work or an illness which affected their ability to completely pay their debts are affected by being charged higher premiums. This is due to the fact that most creditors, even though they work with you, still report you as being late.

Keeping up with your credit is extremely important if you want to maintain lower automobile insurance rates.

Two things that work hand in hand today and really affect your financial security are your credit report and your credit score. You cannot separate one from the other. If one is favorable, then the other would also be favorable. You can not have a favorable credit report and then have a bad credit score because your credit score is based on your report.

Everyone needs to endeavor to keep their credit scores reasonably high and to ensure this, you need to closely monitor your report. not monitoring your credit report well is like handing decisions that have to do with your life to someone else to make for you.

Many times the information submitted to reporting agencies by some business concerning their transaction with you are wrong. This may not in most cases not be a malicious act but it would have the same effect on you unless you quickly identify it and

# How To Raise Your Credit Score

forward a credit bureau dispute letter to the appropriate quarters so the issue can be investigated and corrected.

These days, Banks, lenders, insurance companies amongst other businesses are interested in knowing a person's credit score before determining how to deal with the individual. The rates you would pay on your loan, insurance coverage etc would be seriously affected by your credit score. A low credit score indicates unfavorable financial standing and was you to apply for a loan, you would be considered a high risk and even if your loan is eventually approved, you would pay high rates.

If you checked your credit report and find that there are entries that are in error, you need to have this fully corrected by submitting a credit bureau dispute letter. For those who did not know of this before now or have legally received a judgment on their credit report, you need to work to remove it. A judgment on your credit report can do serious damage to your credit score. The sad part is that when you have received a judgment on your report unless you know what to do or who to turn to for help, you are likely to have this judgment on your credit report for up to 7 years and in all these years, you would be suffering untold financial roadblocks.

You can get help if you want to remove a judgment from your credit report. This is the first step for those who want to remove a judgment. Most people understand that the mortgages that they may qualify for are directly related to their credit scores. Common

## How To Raise Your Credit Score

sense dictates that the better your credit scores are the more mortgages you would qualify for, and for better interest rates, as well. But let's face it, the number of people who have perfect credit is far and few between. Most people have had a mark put on their credit report at one time or another. Some people have had a lot of marks put on them over the years. What can these people do as far as getting good mortgages?

One of the first things you should do before attempting to obtain any type of mortgage is to get your credit reports. There are three major credit reporting agencies, and, by law, you are entitled to a free copy from each one per year. Once you have these reports, you should sit down and carefully review each one to see if there are any mistakes or omissions.

If you find mistakes or omissions, you can write to the agency and request that your information is corrected. It is important to remember that each agency uses only its own information, which means that while one report may be entirely correct, the next may not. This is why you have to go over each one independently.

The reason you want to spend this time investigating your credit reports is that your credit scores are determined by the information on the reports. In order to be fair and accurate, credit scores are determined by set formulas that the agencies use. Erroneous information on your report will cause your scores to drop. This can

# How To Raise Your Credit Score

be a problem when you are looking for mortgages or other types of loans.

In addition to helping you get the best mortgages, you can also help your other credit issues by correcting any mistakes that you find on your reports. Just about all lending agencies use these reports and scores in determining what type of credit and interest rates they will offer you. This includes such things as credit cards, gas cards, and even automobile insurance premiums. As you can see, your credit score can affect much more than just your mortgages.

Another benefit to reviewing your credit reports and credit scores prior to attempting to obtain mortgages is that you may discover that you are in bad shape as far as the numbers go. Some people simply have horrible credit histories and knowing if you fall into that category before you approach a bank or other type lender can be important.

It is important because with very poor marks in your history you may not get a loan at all or you may be offered a sub-prime loan which can become very expensive over time. Knowing, in advance, if you are subject to these types of offers can be helpful.

Sub-prime mortgages will usually carry a much higher interest rate than the traditional fixed rate or ARM loans. The sub-prime market is a market in itself and you need to be very careful before entering into a loan of this nature. Many foreclosures take place within this particular market.

# Chapter 10: What Will Bad Credit Cost You

Having a bad credit score will cost you a lot more than a higher interest rate for a few loans. It extends into many parts of your financial life. So many people fail to understand how important their credit is until they try to buy a home or take out a loan. People with bad credit usually know that they will have to pay higher interest rates. But they often don't realize how deeply they will really be affected.

Let me give you an example. If you have a credit score of 720, you can pretty much expect to get the best rate available. For our example, that is 6%. If you have a credit score that is good but just not perfect -- say 700 -- you could expect to find an interest rate of 6.15%. Not a huge difference. But if you have a credit score of 555, which is considered very poor, you can expect to pay approximately 9.6%. This could result in as much as $500 a month more on a mortgage. That's a lot of money.

In addition to having to pay a higher interest rate, many borrowers with bad credit scores end up paying higher mortgage loan origination fees. To qualify for the much advertised zero percent of low APR financing offered by many car manufacturers, you must have near perfect credit. If you have poor credit, you will

## How To Raise Your Credit Score

probably have to deal with a sub-prime lender (also known as the no-loan is turned down lender). You could pay an interest rate of 25%!

If you already have a bad credit score, a credit card probably isn't a good idea. But it is one of the ways to rebuild your credit. Be prepared to see interest as high 30%, if you can find a credit card at all. You will probably have to pay annual fees as well. Some people are even asked to pay a set-up fee to even get the card. It is often easier to go with a secured card than try to find an unsecured one.

Most people are unaware of the fact that insurance companies use their credit scores to determine risk. The assumption is that people with lower credit scores are at a higher risk for claims than are those with good credit. A person with good credit could pay as much as 10% less than someone with bad credit. This is seen in life insurance, homeowner's insurance, auto insurance and other forms of insurance. Your bad credit can cost you hundreds of dollars a year in insurance premiums.

But that isn't all. You could have to pay a higher deposit to lease or rent an apartment. You could even be turned down for a job. Low credit scores will cost you thousands of extra dollars a year. Take the steps to increase your score. While it isn't easy and it takes time, it is well worth it.

# How To Raise Your Credit Score

## How Much Does Bad Credit Cost?

A man who had been unemployed for two years and had worked as a contractor for three years finally was offered a position in the Department of Defense. The salary offer was supposed $12,000 more than what he is earning as a contractor plus the stability that the job promised. After some bad incidents in his life such as bankruptcy and divorce to his wife, he found hope to start a new life with that offer.

He is Mr. Becraft and he had shared his misfortune caused by bad credit name. Mr. Becraft grabbed the offering so he underwent some background check for him to be employed. However, after he was found to have a history of financial troubles, he was rejected to the job. The reason was he could trade the secret of the nation in exchange for the amount that will set him free from that financial trouble. It was indeed unfair for Mr. Becraft because his skills could prove that he was able to the job. Only that his financial history wasn't favorable or him. And this is just one of the myriad stories of people who lost the job, was not hired even if in all other matters they ualified, or was denied of promotion, again because of bad credit name.

The credit check is not only true to government employers but to any other company workers as well. Employers scrutinize credit histories in order to decide whether he will hire, keep or promote an employee. Yes, bad credit name can cost you your job...and your future!

So, how do you get rid of having a bad credit name? Certainly, the answer is simple: clear your account balance and pay your dues on time. According to surveys, unsettled credits, especially on unpaid credit card balance, can leave a mark on your credit history. You need a good credit name when applying for loans and even for jobs.

Imagine your life when you stumble in an emergency and all you can depend on is an emergency loan which subsequently was denied because of a past financial liability? Especially if the financial trouble all started out with a little amount which hiked because you were not able to settle it down, it would certainly be disheartening. And who should be blamed for this? You. And how do you get rid of these misfortunes with your credit cards?

## Some things to ponder on

Here are some things to ponder on:

You should know that your credit card should give you convenience in procuring goods or paying for services. It should not be used as a means of luxury or expansion of your spending capacity. At the end of the month, you will have to pay for all the purchases you made, so be a wise shopper. Stick to your budget as much as possible so that you are limited to your income capability.

# How To Raise Your Credit Score

In this manner, you avoid unnecessary charges on your account plus your name is cleared in terms of credit credibility.

It is not wise to have a bad credit name if you want to improve yourself in terms of employment. To prove yourself worth the responsibilities, start with clearing your accounts. Make sure that you live within your budget and you will be free from bad credit. Credit is not at all bad, only if you can settle them promptly.

## Difference Between Good Credit And Bad

What is a good credit score is a question anyone who is shopping for a loan will most certainly ask themselves. Knowing what is a good credit score and actually shooting to obtain one can result in some serious financial savings over the lifetime of a loan, so it's a good idea to understand scores and how they impact finances. Not knowing can hurt you.

What is a good credit score will depend a lot on the type of loan involved? In general, however, the determination of what is a good credit score falls in line with the FICO rating. This rating is a number assigned to individuals in regard to their credit. What is a good credit score is often answered by nothing more than the FICO, which stands for Fair Isaac Company, rating? What is a good credit score is determined by this organization that conducts statistical research to measure the probabilities that people will actually repay their loans?

# How To Raise Your Credit Score

The FICO numbers answer the question of what is a good credit score in the form of a range that falls in between 300 and 800 generally. The higher the number, the better, generally. For example, someone with a score of 750 can readily answer the question of what is a good credit score by looking at the types of loan rate offers they obtain. Typically, these people will get very good offers due to their rating.

What is a good credit score is a very important question to ask prior to seeking a big loan. If you find out that the definition of what is a good credit score and your actual score differ greatly, it might be time to repair credit before moving forward. The reason it's important to ask and understand what is a good credit score is vital to ensure you obtain the best possible interest rates on loans. If a score is too low, you will find yourself paying more, sometimes a lot more, over the lifetime of a loan. What is a good credit score will greatly impact the rates offered?

If you find a big disparity between your score and the technical answer to what is a good credit score, you can do some things to help fix the problem. Try to find out what your score is and check out your report. If you find things that are in the report that need to be paid off and fixed, do so.

What is a good credit score can greatly impact your financial future? Knowing what is a good credit score and shooting for one

# How To Raise Your Credit Score

is something anyone who wants to buy a car, a house or even get a credit card should ask and explore.

Credit scores are simply numbers indicating a person's creditworthiness after his credit files were analyzed. Think of it as a student's final grade in school. All his test papers, assignments, quizzes, reports, and attendance factor in the making of his final grade. In a way, it is also derived from various financial transactions such as the payment of bank and car loans, the deals of the house on mortgage, the payment of credit card bills, and other loans such as educational and emergency loans. People who pay their bills on time or in advance receive good credit scores. On the other hand, when people are delinquent in paying their financial obligations, low credit will be given to them.

There is a perfectly reasonable rationale behind making sure that bills are paid on time. Unlike schools grades, credit scores are more than just numbers-it has a bearing on people's future financial dealings so they have to be careful with it. Bad credit will inform future lenders that that particular person is a delinquent payer or that he/she is incapable of paying back loans. This reputation is not good since the lending industry is a business, and it needs to get its money back to be able to make more money out of it. Thus, the most probable result of having low credit scores is that people will be denied their loan applications until they get a more acceptable score in the future.

# How To Raise Your Credit Score

Then again, even if this person simply waits for credit scores to get better, he can't actually get a higher score without adding an entry to his loan history. Say, if he has 420 as his credit score (a very low score in the FICO score range), not borrowing any money from any institution will not make the score go up to 520. People have to incur good credit in order to change their credit score. And this is very difficult to do especially if the person cannot get a loan or is being given a very high-interest rate (another consequence of having bad credit). The higher interest rates that which are given to people with low credit scores is for the purpose of assuring the lenders that they will get their money back even if the borrower defaults on his payments.

So the best way to have healthy financial accounts is to keep the good from the get-go. Bad credit only appear if you let them. If you forget due dates and deadlines often, remind yourself by putting it in your planner or mobile phone reminders. Being a day late in paying bills may not be as bad as a 30-day delay in payment, but still, you are late in paying. Be sure that your salary is enough to pay your bills and your daily necessities. Do not spend more than what you earn because this will eventually lead to financial difficulties in the future. Stay debt free, keep your credit scores high, and you will surely live a better life than your counterparts with bad credit scores.

There has been plenty of talk about good and bad credit scores in the news lately. It is no secret that there plenty of people who have

## How To Raise Your Credit Score

come to the realization that their credit scores are holding them back. The bad credit score is holding them back from owning a home, going to college or even buying a car. So what is a bad credit score? The terms have changed quite a bit over the last decade or so. What used to be considered good has been bumped down to the fair category making it much more difficult for people to obtain prime interest rates on loans.

### 5 things to determine what is a bad credit score versus a good score

Here are 5 things you should know about scores and how to determine what is a bad credit score versus a good score.

- A bad score is somewhat subjective depending on the type of credit a person is applying for. Home loans have some of the strictest credit standards while department store credit cards have fairly lax standards. Home loans will typically consider anything under 640 as a bad score, but that doesn't necessarily mean it is impossible to get a home loan under some programs.
- Credit card companies will often offer credit lines to those with scores ranging in the high 500s and low 600s, but the interest rates will be less than prime. There may be additional fees tacked on as well.
- When talking about what is a bad score, it is important to understand that scores under 500 are considered very bad.

# How To Raise Your Credit Score

People with scores that low will struggle to get unsecured loans or credit lines. However, it isn't the end of the world. It is possible to raise a credit score.

- Unfortunately, it doesn't take much to knock a credit score down. One late payment, bankruptcy, or medical bill sent to the collection can reduce a score by double digits. It takes very little time, a matter of months, in fact, for a score to be negatively impacted, but it can take several months, if not years to repair.

- Consumers with scores that fall into the bad credit range will pay close to double the interest rates compared to those with scores above 640. It is very costly to get an auto loan with interest rates that are essentially punitive. Many consumers would be better served to save the cash in a bank and buy what they need outright rather than take out a high-interest loan.

Understanding how scores impact interest rates for loans and credit cards is an important step to rebuilding credit. Before applying for credit, the consumer must have a firm understanding of what is a bad credit score. Never make assumptions about whether a score is good or bad until you have the facts. Choose wisely when it comes to applying for new credit. Don't get sucked into cards with steep interest rates that will cost you more money and drive you further into debt, effectively hurting your credit score more than it already is.

# How To Raise Your Credit Score

# Chapter 11: Keeping Your Score Healthy

Your credit report is a storyline of your credit life and it is used by potential lenders to determine whether they should provide credit to you. You should be very vigilant of your credit report and maintain it to ensure that a potential future lender will view your financial history favorably when it comes time to lend you the credit you need.

Look at your credit report as if you were the potential lender, would you lend money to yourself? One of the main stories that your credit file will tell you, is how well you keep your commitments. This indicator on your credit report looks at by many people who are weighing upon whether they should invest in you. This is usually done by people who have not known you for a long period of time. This could be a potential employer, a future spouse, a landlord and the credit provider. The credit report is a snapshot in time of your past borrowings and repayments, which also provides a window into your life past the standard financial storyline.

A credit score is a numeric indicator of the risk you are in lending money to. If you have a low score you can find it hard to get credit approved and when you do you could be facing high-interest rates

## How To Raise Your Credit Score

and additional terms and conditions as additional safeguards to the lender. Usually, the lender will want additional insurance taken out on the loan. On the other hand, if you have a high score you will find it easier to obtain credit, with lower rates and without additional terms and conditions from the lender.

The most important actions you can do to ensure that you have a good credit score is to not have too much credit at any one time and to make sure you never fall behind on your repayments, that means you make your repayments before the due date and it would be preferable that you are making additional payments, that way you are in credit on your repayment history. Falling behind in payments is not where you want to be, so do everything possible to make those payments on time, sacrifice something that's not important or mandatory (like that restaurant meal) and make those payments. If you fall behind and are deemed to be delinquent on your loan this will have a big effect on your credit score and subsequently, you will find it hard to get credit in the future. Once you have achieved an excellent credit score you will want to hold onto it. Chances are if you already have the habits developed to help you maintain your score but here is a list of some simple tips that could still help

### 1. Pay Your Bills On Time

There is nothing more important for your FICO score than paying your accounts on time. Your payment history is the largest part of your FICO score and any negative item will have a large impact. You can use methods such as a budget or online bill to help as reminders.

## 2. Don't Apply for Credit Unless You Need

If you have a good standing you will be spammed with an offer for new accounts almost every day. You receive new card offers in the mail offering a low or nonexistent interest rate to apply. Also, every time you go shopping you are offered a discount if you apply for a store account. These limited or one-time discounts are not worth it. If you don't need the credit don't apply for it. Every time you do it will count as an inquiry and this could lower your FICO score.

## 3. Keep Your Balances Low

Your utilization of credit should never exceed 30%. It should sometimes be lower as you balance at any given period of time could be reported to the credit bureaus. If you have not paid your bill, it could register as a higher amount on your report. This gives the impression that you are over 30%.

## 4. Don't Apply for a lot of New Credit in a Short Period of Time

If you do need credit then look around for one credit card, do not apply for every card offer you get in the mail. Also, you are

# How To Raise Your Credit Score

allowed to shop for loans on large purchases such as a mortgage or auto loan. You are given a grace period of 30 days to find a loan. Use this time wisely and do not go over as it will count as a second inquiry.

The last thing you want to do now that you have a good FICO score is lose it. Use your credit wisely and you will maintain and possibly improve.

# Conclusion

Your credit is very important. While it may seem not to matter in your day to day life, the moment you need to buy a big purchase like a car or a house, or even just apply for a new credit card, your credit score can save you a lot of money... or cost you just as much.

The higher your score, the better. A low score can lead to everything from increased interest rates on credit cards and loans to being denied loans altogether. But fortunately, there are a number of ways you can raise your score, or simply keep it high if it's already good.

First off, pay all your bills on time. A history of delinquent payments will hurt your credit score more than anything else. And the shorter your credit history is, the more a single late or missed payment can bring the whole thing down. Just as being late to pay bills lowers your score, paying bills on time and consistently will raise it. But it takes a lot longer to raise your credit score in this manner than to lower it. So be careful, and keep a close eye on those bills, whether it's a minimum payment on your credit card, your monthly internet bill, or even just a parking ticket. If you can help it at all, never, ever let a bill go to collections because that will be a black mark on your credit report for a long time.

# How To Raise Your Credit Score

Also, don't let your debt get out of hand. Having a small balance on a credit card or two won't hurt you, and if consistently paid off will actually help your score, but owing more money than you conceivably have to multiple creditors will reflect badly on you. This is generally good advice anyway, but it's particularly relevant to raising your credit score. If you can afford it, paying off all your debts will help your credit score, and at least making the minimum payments is a must.

So basically, pay off your bills and try to keep yourself out of debt. If you're thinking of applying for a loan soon and your credit isn't all that great, it will probably pay off to wait on applying for that loan until you've spent some time trying to improve your credit. And if you really, really need help, and can afford it, hiring a credit counselor is a good way to raise your score rapidly. But hopefully, just by following these common-sense guidelines... and not falling on particularly hard times... you should be able to keep your credit score healthy and high. Good luck.

Credit means everything in today's world. It affects a person's ability to buy a car, a home and even insurance rates. With so much emphasis placed on good credit, it is imperative a person knows how to raise your credit score. With a good credit score, which is typically defined as a score above at least 650, moderate interest rates on credit cards and loans are offered. This can save a great deal of money in the long run. These 5 tips will help increase

## How To Raise Your Credit Score

a score and afford a person the luxury of more credit with better rates.

1. Pay every bill on time even if the payment sent is just the minimum amount due. One late payment can dramatically reduce a credit score. It doesn't matter if it is only a day late. Late is late and it will negatively impact the overall score. If a payment absolutely must be late, contact the creditor and ask for an extension. Most companies will offer to do this once a year.
2. Avoid having a bill sent to collections. Even if the bill is paid off, the collection report will stay on a credit report for seven years. Work with a creditor to arrange monthly payments before a bill is sent to collections. Most creditors will accept monthly payments as long as the payments are made on time every month.
3. Avoid paying off all credit card balances completely. If you want to know how to raise your credit score, it is best to have a balance on credit accounts that monthly payments are made to. This proves the ability to maintain regular payments and will help to increase a credit score.
4. It is crucial a person pays close attention to his or her credit report. Any unauthorized charges should be disputed immediately. This can also be an indicator of identity theft. As soon as a suspicious account appears on a credit report, it should be investigated immediately.

## How To Raise Your Credit Score

5. Avoid closing accounts that are not currently in use. Scores depend heavily on credit history. Pull out an old credit card and use it for minor purchases from time to time to keep it active. The older a credit history, the better it is for a credit score.

These tips are some of the easiest for a person to implement. The tips provided will help improve a score in a matter of months. For those who have a goal to buy a new car or a home, it is a good idea to start working on improving a credit score at least six months to a year before applying for a loan. This ensures the best rates and gives plenty of time to work on getting negative marks removed while ensuring regular payments are being made. When you are trying to find out how to improve your credit score, be wary of programs that charge a lot of money before any work is done.

The things that affect your credit score include charge off's, collections and negatives that were not yours in the first place, late payments, low credit limits reported, accounts listed as paid as agreed, paid derogatory, paid charge-off or settled, accounts listed as unpaid and lastly, negative items that have occurred over a seven-period. How to raise your credit score will not happen overnight so you have to pay your bills on time, check your credit limits and make sure previous loans have been settled. That way, there won't be a problem when a lender conducts a background check on your credit history and your loan can be approved.

www.ingramcontent.com/pod-product-compliance
Lightning Source LLC
Chambersburg PA
CBHW070203230526
45471CB00002B/802